THERE ARE

NO
ANIMALS

IN THIS BOOK!

(ONLY FEELINGS)

For Nika, my inspiration.

With heartfelt appreciation for each of the artists whose
generosity helped make this book possible.

THERE ARE NO ANIMALS IN THIS BOOK! (ONLY FEELINGS)

Story © 2013 Chani Sanchez
Appendix text © 2013 Chani Sanchez and Tina Rivers

Published by POW!
a division of powerHouse Packaging & Supply, Inc.

Library of Congress Control Number: 2013937981

37 Main Street, Brooklyn, NY 11201-1021
info@bookPOW.com
www.bookPOW.com
www.powerHouseBooks.com
www.powerHousePackaging.com

ISBN: 978-1-57687-644-2

Book and Cover design by Peter Sunna and J. Longo
Jacket design by J. Longo and Peter Sunna

Typeset in Brauer Neu

10 9 8 7 6 5 4 3 2 1

Printed in Malaysia

THERE ARE NO ANIMALS IN THIS BOOK!

(ONLY FEELINGS)

CHANI SANCHEZ

AHEM...

THIS IS A BOOK ABOUT FEELINGS.

(NOT ANIMALS.)

WAIT, NOT ABOUT ANIMALS? WHY?

Cow, 2006 by Alex Katz

BECAUSE

EVERYONE ALREADY KNOWS A COW SAYS MOO!

BUT DID YOU KNOW THAT FEELINGS SAY THINGS, TOO?

DID YOU KNOW THAT . . .

SAD SAYS WHAAA!

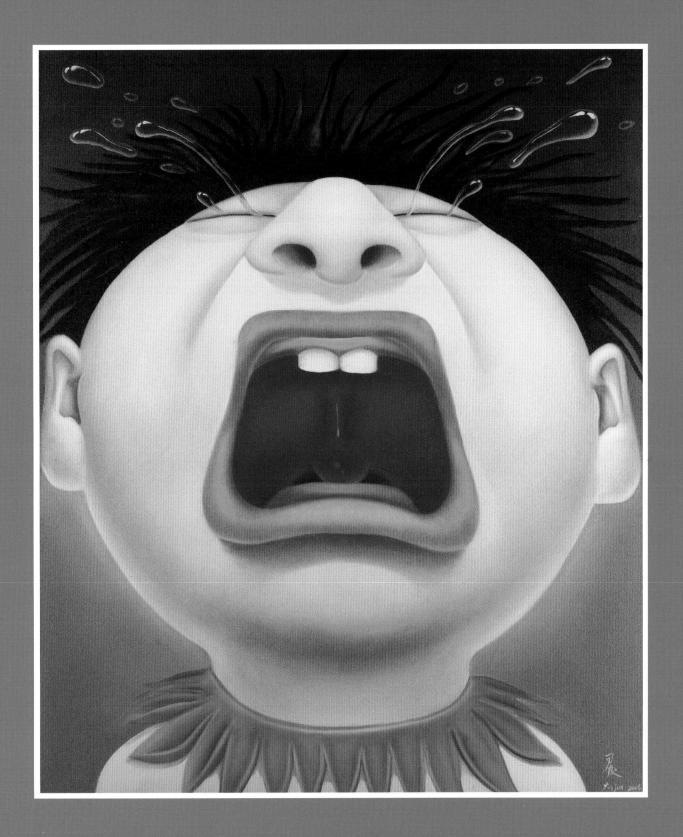

Crying, 2006 by Yin Jun

Rainbow Flower—11 O'Clock, 2007 by Takashi Murakami

HAPPY
SAYS
YAY!

ANGRY
SAYS
GRRRR!

Divine Warrior fragment, 2005 by Judy Fox

A PONY
SAYS
NEIGH!

WAIT! A PONY?   UMMM, I THINK I ALREADY MENTIONED
THERE ARE <u>NO ANIMALS</u> IN THIS BOOK!

NOW WHERE WAS I?   OH, YES...

The Call of the Continent, 2006 by Donald Baechler

LOVE
SAYS
MMMM!

World 4, 2005 by Ruud van Empel

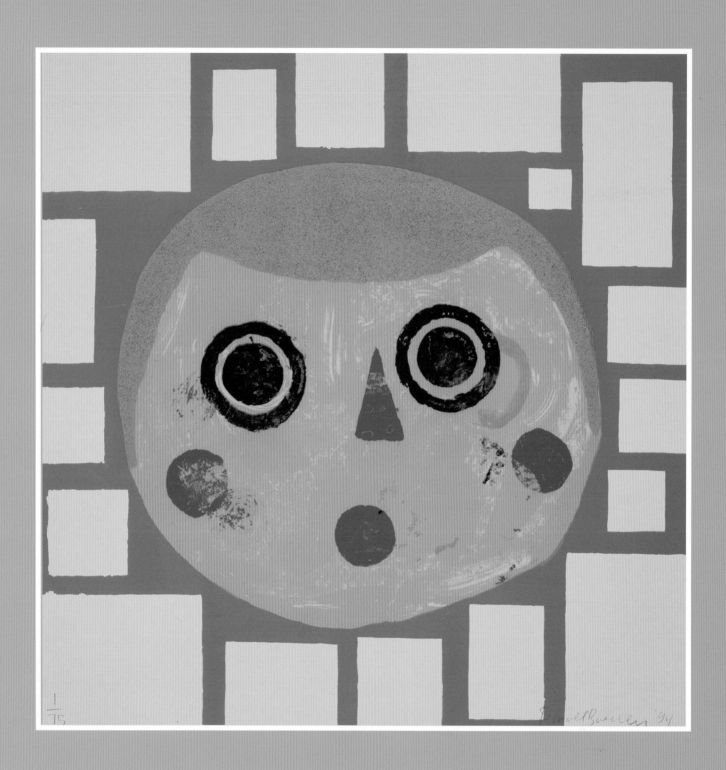

1/75

Coney Island V, 1994 by Donald Baechler

SURPRISE
SAYS

LONELY SAYS BRRRR!

Snow White, 2006 by Liu Ye

CRANKY SAYS

NO!

Wo ist Verantwortung fur eine Welt, 1993 by Yoshitomo Nara

HURT
SAYS
OWWW!!

Untitled, 2003 by Tom Friedman

A CAT SAYS

MEOWWW!

A <u>CAT</u>???

LOOK, I'M JUST GOING TO SAY GOODBYE
IF YOU ANIMALS WON'T CUT IT OUT.

Hello Kitty, 2002 by Tom Sachs

WAIT! WE HAVE FEELINGS, TOO!

AND BEING LEFT OUT IS MAKING US SAD!

Winter Bears, 1988 by Jeff Koons

MAKING YOU SAD?

THAT MAKES ME SAD!

WHAT IF I SAID:

ANIMALS

CAN

BE IN THIS BOOK?

HOORAY!

THAT WOULD MAKE US FEEL OVERJOYED!

(WHICH IS LIKE HAPPY TIMES A MILLION!) BUT...

An Homage to Yves Klein, Multicolor B, 2012 by Takashi Murakami

WE CAN'T CALL IT

"THERE ARE NO

ANIMALS

IN THIS BOOK"

IF THERE ARE ANIMALS!

Papilio Ulysses, 2008 by Damien Hirst

WHAT **IF** WE CALL IT

" THERE ARE NO

ROBOTS

IN THIS BOOK "

INSTEAD?

WAIT, NO **ROBOTS** IN THIS BOOK?

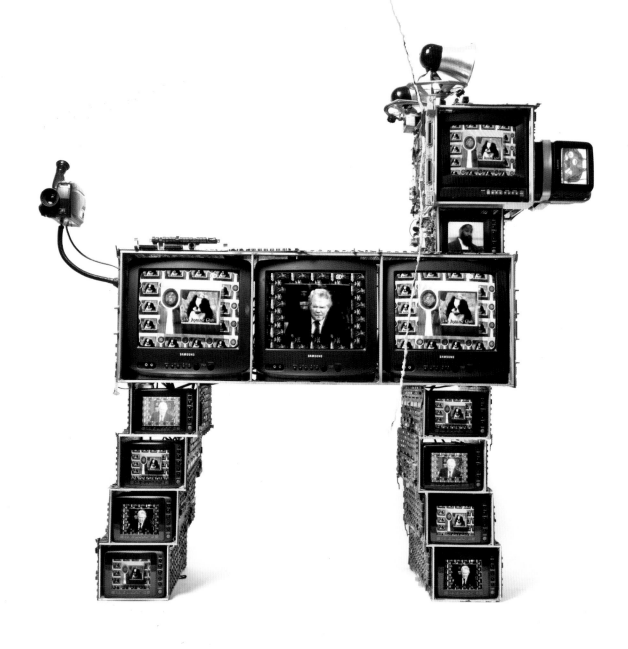

Watchdog II, 1997 by Nam June Paik

OH, NO! NOT AGAIN!

THE END.

Cow, 2006 by Alex Katz
Silkscreen on aluminum cutout, 47½ x 72⅜ inches (120 x 180 cm)
Photography by Paul Takeuchi. Art © Alex Katz/Licensed by VAGA, NY, NY

In Cow, we see Katz's interest in the familiar styles of advertising and fashion at play, as a farm animal is humorously transformed into a glamorous and expressionless model. In the 1950s, Katz rejected the raw emotionality of abstract expressionism (embodied, for example, by the work of Jackson Pollock) and embraced the everyday look of mainstream visual culture, thereby foreshadowing the rise of Pop Art.

Crying, 2006 by Yin Jun
Oil on canvas, 47¼ x 39⅜ inches (118 x 98 cm)
Courtesy Beijing Central Art Gallery, Michelle Rosenfeld Gallery, and Sotheby's © Yin Jun

As in all of Jun's works, this painting offers an extremely exaggerated portrait of an emotional child (or infantilized adult) whose tears shoot into the air above a gaping, bellowing mouth. The sadness and frustration of Jun's somewhat grotesque characters—who often are shown playing games or eating cake while they cry—suggest both the harrowing living conditions for many in China and the suffering caused by an increasingly materialistic world where emotional pain is not vanquished by new luxuries.

Rainbow Flower–11 O'Clock, 2007 by Takashi Murakami
Acrylic and platinum leaf on canvas mounted on board, 15¾ inches (39 cm) diameter
© 2012 Takashi Murakami/Kaikai Kiki Co., Ltd. All Rights Reserved

At first glance, the saccharine rainbow colors and wide smile of this anthropomorphic flower radiate joy and friendliness; but if you keep looking, the unchanging expression starts to seem forced, or even troubled. While playing with Japanese culture's rampant obsession with *kawaii*, or "cuteness," Murakami undercuts his works' cartoonish sweetness with a tinge of irony. Ultimately, this strategy reveals the very thing *kawaii* supposedly hides: the trauma of WWII and its aftermath.

Divine Warrior fragment, 2005 by Judy Fox
Aqua-resin and casein, 10 x 7 x 5 inches (25 x 17.5 x 12.5 cm)
Courtesy of the artist and P.P.O.W Gallery, New York © Judy Fox

From its glowing skin and shining eyes to its aggressive, archaic hairstyle, this sculpted head painted with casein fancifully captures the stubborn defiance of a child "warrior." Fox typically works in clay, a prehistoric art medium, and draws upon time-worn fairy-tales and mythologies; the resulting images breathe life into ancient forms and ideas, especially regarding children and women.

The Call of the Continent, 2006 by Donald Baechler
Acrylic and fabric collage on canvas, 111 x 144 inches (281.9 x 365.8 cm)
© 2013 Donald Baechler/Artists Rights Society (ARS), New York

One of the New York artists of the 1980s associated with the revival of figurative art, Baechler intensely labors over his canvases, building them up with layers of paint, fabric, and images imported from mass-produced visual culture. In his "Horses" series, awkward black-and-white drawings of flattened horses, reminiscent of those found in vintage children's books, float over a groundless grid of visual flotsam. Evoking a patchwork narrative and a sense of childhood memory, the work marries figuration to abstraction, painting to drawing, and art to craft.

World 4, 2005 by Ruud van Empel
Cibachrome, 23 1/25 x 33 1/9 inches (59.4 x 84.1 cm)
Courtesy Flatland Gallery (Amsterdam, Paris) © Ruud van Empel

This shimmering photograph from van Empel's acclaimed "World" series comprises dozens of individual shots of the flora, the girl, and her toy, including individual parts of her face and dress. Working much like a painter, but using Photoshop as his tool instead of a paintbrush, van Empel layered these fragments to create a seamless, hyper-real image of a lush but artificial primordial world, challenging our expectations of photographic realism.

Coney Island V, 1994 by Donald Baechler
10-color screenprint with sand, 29 x 29 inches (74 x 74 cm)
© 2013 Donald Baechler/Artists Rights Society (ARS), New York

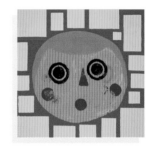

As in a child's doodle (or early digital art), this face is depicted using only basic geometric forms and unmodulated bright colors; its ruddy cheeks and wide eyes and mouth also lend it an air of innocence. Perhaps this naive figure is surprised at being framed and complemented by squares and rectangles, which, though simple, make reference not only to the busy landscape of Coney Island, but also to the unique styles of two of modern art's most prominent forefathers—Malevich and Mondrian.

Snow White, 2006 by Liu Ye
Acrylic and oil on canvas, 82 5/8 x 82 5/8 inches (209.9 x 209.9 cm)
Private Collection, Courtesy Sperone Westwater, New York © Liu Ye

Ye's secret reading of stories by Hans Christian Andersen as a boy growing up in Maoist China inspired him to become an artist. By setting solitary figures like Snow White and Pinocchio, and even Anderson himself, against indistinct backgrounds, Ye captures childhood feelings of loneliness, while suggesting the paradoxical universality of those feelings. His painterly style similarly unites the volumetric fullness of European painting with the anatomical distortions of Japanese cartooning.

Wo ist Verantwortung fur eine Welt, 1993 by Yoshitomo Nara
Acrylic on canvas, 59 1/10 x 59 1/10 inches (148 x 148 cm) © Yoshitomo Nara

Fueled by his lonely childhood in rural Japan, Nara, a leader of "Tokyo Pop," makes images of children who are not darling innocents, but rebellious rabble-rousers—even sticking their tongues out at the adults who (literally) look down at them. The artworks are rebellious, too, walking the line between casualness and calculation: here, the flat colors and bold, simple lines belie the careful rhyming of the girl's tongue with her pigtails, and of her bulbous head and body with the tiny "world" on which she stands, triumphant.

Untitled, 2003 by Tom Friedman
Trash can, paper, 60 1/2 x 39 x 37 inches (151 x 97.5 x 92.5 cm)
Courtesy of the artist, Luhring Augustine, New York, and Stephen Friedman Gallery, London © Tom Friedman

In Untitled, Friedman, a conceptual sculptor, uses his trademark everyday materials (here, construction paper, glue, and a trash can) to create a darkly humorous tableau. Friedman's work is highly personalized, and this work reflects his emotional catharsis as he "throws himself away" in the aftermath of a painful experience. While his obvious discomfort invites our sympathy, the "V" shape made by the legs reminds us of the sign for "victory" and the hope of a better tomorrow.

Hello Kitty, 2002 by Tom Sachs
Bronze with ink and white patina, 7 x 5 x 6 inches (17.5 x 12.5 x 15 cm)
Engraved with signature, numbered and dated "Tom Sachs H.C. 2001" on underside of base.
From an edition of 25 plus five artist's proofs. Courtesy Sperone Westwater, New York and Phillip's New York © Tom Sachs

Sachs is a sculptor and installation artist who recreates familiar icons and environments, from the inside of a McDonald's to the bridge of the USS *Enterprise*. By sculpting the kitschy but beloved Hello Kitty character in expensive bronze that was painted white to look like the cheap foam model from which it was cast, Sachs prompts us to think about the value—financial, emotional, and otherwise—that we assign to our popular icons and to art.

Winter Bears, 1988 by Jeff Koons
Polychromed wood, 48 x 44 x 15 ½ inches (121.9 x 111.8 x 39.4 cm) © Jeff Koons

As in most of his work, Koons here takes a banal object and alters it not only by placing it in an art context, but also by having it meticulously recreated on a larger scale. Its new size and unequalled level of craftsmanship (manufactured using the methods of Medieval church sculptors) thus reflects the original owners' emotional investment in their trinket. But does this work celebrate "lowbrow" taste, or does it criticize the affection lavished on knickknacks like these (instead of on "Art")?

An Homage to Yves Klein, Multicolor B, 2012 by Takashi Murakami
Acrylic and platinum leaf on canvas mounted on aluminum frame
30⁷¹/₁₀₀ x 22⁴/₂₅ inches, (77 x 55 cm) Courtesy Galerie Emmanuel Perrotin, Paris
© 2012 Takashi Murakami/Kaikai Kiki Co., Ltd. All Rights Reserved.

Despite his reputation as a Neo-Pop artist who presides over his own Warhol-esque "Factory," Murakami is highly trained in *nihonga*, or traditional Japanese painting. This "homage to Yves Klein," a post-war avant-garde artist who made monochrome paintings with his own patented shade of blue, copies the "all-over" homogenous pictorial field of monochrome painting; but rather than fill the surface with one color, Murakami uses his iconic happy flowers, which obliquely refer to the heritage of Japanese landscape painting. These different traditions have influenced Murakami's style, which mirrors the kaleidoscopic global condition of art today.

Monkey Train (Birds), 2007 by Jeff Koons
Oil on canvas, 108 x 84 inches (274.3 x 213.4 cm) © Jeff Koons

The smiling monkey face at the center of this canvas was copied by Koons' assistants from a photo of an inflatable monkey that could have been purchased anywhere, perhaps at a fair or a party supply store. While Koons sometimes seems to celebrate the everyday objects he recreates, by placing the cartoonish monkey on top of photos of real birds and silhouettes of trains and carriages here, Koons sets our mainstream, mass-produced culture against both nature and history, which have become "flattened" in its wake.

Papilio Ulysses, 2008 by Damien Hirst
Butterflies and household gloss on canvas, 84 x 84 inches (210 x 210 cm)
Photographed by Prudence Cuming Associates
© Damien Hirst and Science Ltd. All rights reserved, DACS 2013

In his "Butterfly Paintings," Hirst—an artist renowned for his provocative works—makes images of butterflies using actual butterflies and paint. The beautiful results look like mosaics or stained glass windows, and just as those works of art can inspire spiritual feelings in their viewers, Hirst's fragile surfaces prod us to consider how artists, much like butterfly collectors, attempt to "capture" our transitory world.

Watchdog II, 1997 by Nam June Paik
Aluminum framework, circuit boards, intercom horns, audio speakers, Panasonic camcorder,
desk lamp, three 13" Samsung TVs model TXD 1372, one 9" KEC TV model 9BND, nine 5" Magnavox TVs
62 x 67 x 19 inches (155 x 167.5 x 47.5 cm) © Nam June Paik Studios and Christie's Images Limited 2010

In the 1960s, Paik–who is considered by many to be the father of video art–pioneered the use of televisions and electronic hardware in the creation of art forms suited to the dawning information age. In *Watchdog II*, Paik "domesticates" technology by combining TVs and other hardware with the instantly recognizable form of our loyal companion, the dog, while playing with the idea of who is "watching" whom. Through these and other projects, Paik transformed technology into an artist's medium, and in so doing, showed us not only what art could be, but also what our world would become.